Hare and Tortoise Have Counselling

Maria 彗 Claridge

ISBN-13: 979-8-6339-1091-9

DEDICATION

I dedicate this book to all readers wanting to know more about the different types of counselling.

ACKNOWLEDGMENTS

I would like to give special thanks to my dearest friend Alistair.

I would also like to thank my family, friends and Daisuke, for their support and input.

Material and inspiration from my 'CPCAB Diploma in Therapeutic Counselling TC-L4' course, Redland Counselling and Training.

INTRODUCTION

This is a story based on the characters from the Aesop's Fable, 'The Hare and Tortoise.' For those who are unfamiliar with the story, Hare and Tortoise decide to have a race. In the race Hare decides to take a nap, allowing Tortoise to overtake him and win.

1
HARE AND TORTOISE

HARE

It wasn't supposed to be this way for Hare. Growing up, he felt under pressure to stand out in his family. His father would always comment on how he wished for one of his children to make the family proud, how he wished for one of them to rise to superstardom and bring glory to the household.

Hare's parents prided themselves on constant success. His father was a championship runner, a legend in the racing world, with a lifetime's worth of gold medals won at the International Rat Race – the most prestigious race in the Animal Kingdom. His mother was a successful athlete herself and had gained many sponsorships and endorsements. In her prime, she could be seen in adverts drinking the popular sports drink, Carrot-ade.

Hare's siblings were no slouches, either. His brothers and sisters pursued different athletic endeavours and they were all highly successful, filling Hare's parents with pride.

Hare had always felt pressure. But Hare was the only runner in his generation of the family. This meant that he was the only one that had a shot at maintaining his parents' legacy of excellence in events. Whether it was said explicitly or not, he felt the weight on his shoulders every day.

Hare loved running. It was the only thing he felt good about. Teachers, friends and siblings had told Hare that he wasn't very clever, but he was good at running. He struggled through school and just barely managed to get into his last-choice university, a result that would have been more closely scrutinised had a full athletic scholarship not followed. In Hare's eyes, his athletic prowess was all he had to give.

All eyes were on him in his race against Tortoise, a race in which he was a huge favourite.

TORTOISE

It wasn't supposed to be this way for Tortoise, either. He had somehow made it into the running team, but he always suspected that he was just there to make up the numbers. His coach had only ever paid perfunctory attention to his lap times and barely took notice of his improving times over the years. Regardless of how much effort and time he had put into the track, he had always been shrugged off as some cute little creature that never really had a chance.

His family wasn't much help, either. The first time he brought up the idea of running with his father, he was laughed from the dinner table. His father told him 'Son, there is no point in competing! With such short legs and a big, heavy shell'. As the months went on his mother, although a little bit kinder would often ask if he was going to move on. 'Forget about running darling, get yourself a sensible hobby for a tortoise, you'll be happier and that'll make me happier,' she would say.

This a toxic combination was what he had lived with for longer than he could remember. All his life, he heard, 'You can't do it,' or 'It's impossible,' ringing through his head.

He worked hard work over the years to improve himself and get to where he was. Yet despite all this, there always seemed to be a cloud hanging over his head, a voice telling him that he was not good enough and that he would never amount to anything.

2
THE RACE

Stunned, the crowd stared in silence. The race was won but their favourite, Hare, was nowhere in sight.

A sudden eruption of cheering and whistling. The animals began to crowd around Tortoise, to congratulate him on the huge upset. 'Well done, Tortoise! My oh my, did not see that coming! You showed Hare!' said all the other animals.

Tortoise returned the smiles, stunned himself at his unexpected victory. But, despite winning the race, Tortoise did not himself feel the enthusiasm of the crowd. He felt no joy. Instead, his stomach felt in a knot.

As Hare caught sight of the crowd surrounding Tortoise, his ears drooped. His heart sank to the ground. He turned around and headed straight home.

3

HARE

Harriet, the youngest in Hare's family, was concerned about her big brother. He had not been attending their regular Sunday family dinners and on her daily commute to school, she had not spotted him running.

One day she decided to drop by Hare's home. As she approached the doorstep, she noticed that all his curtains were closed.

'This is odd,' she thought. She knocked. No answer. She tried the door.

Surprised, she found it open. 'Maybe he went away and forgot to lock up,' she pondered. She stepped into the dark living space.

'Brother Hare?' There was no reply. She called out a little louder. 'Brother Hare?'

She opened the door into his bedroom to find Hare smothered under blankets in darkness. 'Brother Hare!' she exclaimed, rushing to his side. Harriet felt panicked. The usually bright and tidy home was dark and messy. Clothes, books, food wrappers and all manner of random objects were strewn about the room. There was an odd smell and she soon realised that Hare had not been bathing. 'Brother Hare, what's wrong?'

VISITING DOCTOR DUCK

After much persuading from Harriet, who called on Hare each day, Hare finally agreed to go see the doctor with her. They eventually agreed that this would be the best way forward. Harriet was beginning to feel overwhelmed by not knowing how to help her brother.

Harriet stayed in the waiting room as Hare went in to see the doctor. Straightaway the doctor noticed Hare's slim frame and the large bags under his eyes. 'Hello Hare, what brings you here today?' the doctor asked, smiling reassuringly.

'I haven't been feeling very well,' said Hare.

'Where have you not been feeling well?' There was silence. Hare could not bear to look the doctor in the eyes and instead stared off into the corner of the ceiling. The doctor prompted, 'Head? Stomach...?' He smiled at Hare trying to offer some reassurance.

'My body is heavy... and my mind, doc...' Hare paused. 'My mind feels particularly heavy.'

The doctor furrowed his eyebrows with a look of concern. 'Hare, would you fill in this PHQ-9 form? This will give me an indication on your health and wellbeing.'

Hare took the form and began reading the questions to himself. 'Little pleasure or interest in doing things?' Hare circled, 'Nearly every day'.

'In the past two weeks, how often have you felt down, depressed, or hopeless?' Hare again circled, 'Nearly every day'.

'Are you feeling bad about yourself, feeling you have let yourself or your family down?' Hare felt his heart sink. A wave of guilt started spreading through his whole body. Another circle on 'Nearly every day.' And so, the questions went on.

The doctor analysed the results and concluded that Hare was suffering from depression and, if left much longer, it could become dangerous. 'Hare, you are suffering from depression,' he said.

Puzzled, Hare looked at the doctor for the first time.

The doctor went on. 'Depression is a common medical illness that negatively affects how you feel, the way you think and how you act. Fortunately, it's also treatable.'

Hare tilted his head. 'Depression?'

The doctor gave Hare some time to digest the idea, then continued, 'Before exploring the option of antidepressants, I would like to recommend you to a Cognitive Behavioural Therapist, "CBT", counsellor named Crow. I think it's important to make an appointment as soon as possible.' The doctor turned to his computer to compose an email. 'Now, does tomorrow at 10 a.m. suit you?'

Hare felt like he had no choice. 'I guess …'

'Good. I'll have it arranged,' the doctor replied. On a piece of paper, the Doctor scribbled down the address. 'Here you are.' He handed Hare the piece of paper.

'Thank you,' Hare said meekly, still unable to look the doctor in the eye, despite his best efforts.

As Hare left, the doctor felt troubled. He had known Hare since he was young and had seen in the local newspaper how Hare had lost the race to Tortoise. The story had gone viral and poor Hare had been harassed at his home by reporters for many days after. No one had really seen him out since then. He was not altogether surprised to hear that Hare had stayed at home all that time. He knew that this was not normal for a hare who before had been active and happy. His brows furrowed as he finished his email to Crow about his concerns for Hare. He took special care to mention the dire situation he felt Hare was in.

THE CBT COUNSELLOR CROW

For the first time since the race, Hare got up before midday. He felt grotty and weak and he wanted to cancel the appointment. In the end though, the thought of breaking his promise to Harriet was enough to get him to step out the front door.

'Hello Hare,' said Crow.

Hare nodded. But had no smile. His fur was unkempt and his shoulders were slumped. This did not go unnoticed by Crow. 'I understand that this is your first time seeing a counsellor?'

Hare nodded slowly. As he had been with the doctor, he could not bring himself to look Crow in the eyes. He wore the same sad expression.

'Everything we discuss is private and confidential. We will have a total of six sessions. We will meet once a week at the same time and on the same day.'

Again, Hare nodded slowly, thinking that six weeks was a long time.

Crow asked 'Do you know anything about CBT?'

Hare shrugged his shoulders and responded, 'I think it stands for Cognitive Behavioural Therapy?'

'Yes, you and I work together to change an attitude or behaviour by focusing on your thoughts and beliefs. We explore your thought processes, and how they relate to the way you think and behave.'

Hare took some time to digest this information. 'So, we will be looking at my thoughts.'

'Yes, we will, Hare. This is the time you have put aside to invest in yourself.' Crow paused then continued with a quote from Burns. 'If you are willing to invest a little time in yourself, you can learn to master your moods more effectively, just as an athlete who participates in a daily conditioning program can develop greater endurance and strength.'

Hare made eye contact with Crow for the first time since entering the room. Something in Crow's analogy interested him.

'CBT focuses on current issues and thoughts. Can you tell me what you've been thinking?' Crow asked.

There was a short silence. Hare looked down, feeling ashamed. 'I've been feeling like I'm not myself these days. I struggle to get up. I struggle to eat. I struggle to leave the house. The doctor said I was depressed. I'm not really sure what this means ... '

'Depression is the constant thinking of negative thoughts, Hare.'

'How do we treat it?'

'It's about challenging those thoughts,' explained Crow.

'It's so overwhelming.'

'Okay, let's break this down. Together, we will create practical ways to improve your state of mind each day.'

'Together,' thought Hare. 'I am not alone.' He felt the weight of that word, 'Together.' Something about it felt calming to him. He adjusted his posture, sitting slightly straighter and less slouched than when he first entered the room.

The session ended and Hare left with homework assigned to him by Crow. He was to keep a mood journal which meant he was going to write about his daily activities and note his moods as he was doing them, using a scale of one to ten.

'Just use a word, summing up how you feel.' Crow said kindly.

For the first time since losing the race, Hare felt a glimmer of hope.

CBT SESSION TWO

Hare was surprised how diligent he had been over his homework. After spending the week documenting his daily movements, he realised how little he was doing every day. Homework in hand and feeling nervous, Hare took a deep breath as he entered Crow's room. He had no idea what to expect going into his second session. What was Crow going to say about his daily activities of – not so much?

All the nerves he was feeling before the session dissipated when he entered the room. Inside, Crow greeted him with a warm smile. 'Hello Hare.'

'Hello Crow.' Hare looked at Crow, straight in the eyes this time. Crow made a mental note of the positive change.

Crow also noted that Hare had greeted him this time. 'Let's take a look at your homework together,' Crow invited. 'Why don't you start by telling me about Monday?'

Hare went on to go through day after day with Crow. He reported low scores on his mood levels. He was sleeping through most of his days.

'What were you thinking here?' Crow asked, pointing to midday on Saturday on Hare's homework sheet.

'I was hoping that the ground would swallow me up,' Hare confessed.

'Would you not miss your friends and family if that were to happen?' Crow challenged.

'My mother and father would not notice.'

Something had shifted in the atmosphere. The mention of Hare's parents added a weight in the air that wasn't previously there. Crow noted the shift mentally and then continued, 'I understand it was your youngest sister who got you to seek help?'

'Yes, that was Harriet.' Harriet, his beloved sister, had been over every day with casseroles and carrot cake, Hare's favourite. She had been tidying his home and confided in him all the ins and outs of her life at school. Hare thought about how worried she had looked when she had first found him under the covers. He could never leave Harriet. She had always brought him so much joy. 'Yes. I would miss Harriet.'

They continued the session, going through his mood journal, breaking down his negative thoughts and Hare described his feelings. The session went by much quicker than first time.

'Okay Hare, thank you for this. I'd like for you to continue with your homework. On top of that, I have a new piece of homework for you. I'd like you to try five minutes of movement each day.'

'That doesn't seem so hard. I think I can manage that!' Hare replied. Before losing the race to Tortoise, he had been a daily runner. 'I can do this,' Hare told himself.

'Now this could be gentle stretching, or just walking outside around the house. Remember, there is no pressure. No goals to hit. Just enjoy the experience and try to be present in the moment.'

'What do you mean by, present in the moment?'

'Notice what you are seeing and experiencing in that very moment' smiled Crow.

'Okay,' replied Hare.

'Good. See you at the same time next week.'

MINDFULNESS

In session three, Crow explained mindfulness. They did an exercise where Crow brought in a leaf. They looked at the leaf, explored the colour of the leaf and talked a bit about the life of the leaf.

Hare found the exercise silly at first, but as he noticed the swirls of green and orange mixed, he could not help but see the leaf's beauty. The exercise was calming.

Crow set the homework of practicing mindfulness each day. 'It doesn't need to be long, just take your time; be more aware of things you encounter daily,' Crow said.

Harriet and Hare went home for dinner together. Hare tried eating slower and asked about the ingredients that Harriet had used. He found himself more grateful for the food. The experience of eating was much more enjoyable. He was so accustomed to thinking food was nothing but fuel for the body, that he could not remember the last time he sat and enjoyed his food for the sake of it.

THE ABC EXERCISE

In the next session, Crow had an ABC worksheet ready for Hare. 'Hello, Hare, take a look at this. In the middle of the worksheet is a box labelled Behaviours.'

Hare looked at the empty box.

'In this box, you write down any potentially problematic behaviours you want to analyse.'

Hare began writing down his constant need to sleep, his lack of appetite and not wanting to socialise.

'Now,' said Crow. 'On the left side of the worksheet is a box labelled 'Antecedents,' in which you note down the factors that preceded a behaviour.'

Hare felt puzzled and Crow sensed this. 'These are factors that led up to the behaviour under consideration, either directly or indirectly.'

Hare wrote down three words in big, bold letters. 'LOSING THE RACE.'

'Good. On the right side is the final box labelled 'Consequences'. This is where you write down what happened as a result of the behaviour under consideration.'

'I lost everything,' Hare murmured.

'Hare, consequences may sound inherently negative, but that's not necessarily the case. Some positive consequences can arise from many types of behaviours.'

Hare wrote down the negative consequences. Over-sleeping left him unable to sleep throughout the night. It left him feeling agitated. His lack of appetite had left him feeling weak. His lack of socialising had made him feel very lonely. He felt very uncertain about his future making him anxious. But on a positive note, he had been spending more time with Harriet.

Crow talked through these behaviours with Hare and he realised he could no longer continue these negative behaviours. It was time for change.

ACCEPTING UNCERTAINTY

'Next week will be our last session Hare. You have mentioned uncertainties and how this has added to your anxiety. Maybe we can come up with a solution.'

'I know what the solution is,' said Hare confidently. 'The solution to fighting uncertainty is accepting uncertainty.'

'Yes Hare. By choosing to willingly tolerate not knowing how situations will turn out, we expend less energy fighting unnecessary battles, getting tied up in knots about things in unhelpful ways. Acceptance does not necessarily mean enjoying uncertainty. It merely means acknowledging that there is a degree of the unknown in everything we do and letting go of the fight with reality.'

Hare nodded, amazed by what Crow's was saying.

'The following exercises are food for thought. I would like you to go away and think about the following questions.'

'Okay,' said Hare.

'First of all, let us weigh the pros and cons of accepting uncertainty.'

'Pro, well I can't think of any ... maybe I have a reason to not get out of bed?' asked Hare.

'Next, let us Identify areas of your life in which you're already accepting of uncertainty.'

'My running future is very uncertain.'

'Think smaller, for example getting stuck at the crossing on your way here.'

'I'm going to the new cafe with Harriet tomorrow, that is an uncertainty.'

'Good example. Take a moment to consider how accepting some degree of uncertainty is helpful in these situations, and take the same attitude with more difficult areas of your life'

'Okay.'

'Analyse what underlying meaning uncertainty has for you.'

'What does this mean?'

'Sometimes, without being aware of it, we automatically associate uncertainty with a negative outcome. If you do this, take a step back from this way of thinking and really ascertain whether there's any evidence for it. Take another moment and identify the evidence against this assumption. Chances are, by thinking about uncertainty from this new perspective, it may seem less threatening.'

'Ah, I see.'

'Finally, imagine what life would look like without uncertainty.'

'How?" exclaimed Hare.

'Don't you think that too much certainty would make life pretty dull? How enjoyable would conversations be if you knew exactly what the other animal was going to say?'

'I always know exactly how my father will respond.'

Crow noticed Hare's shift in mood. She decided to move the conversation, but mentally noted what triggered the shift.

'With absolute certainty, there would be no pleasant surprises. Think when Harriet surprised you with the carrot cake.'

'Yes, this is true.'

'So, the next time you tense up with a feeling of uncertainty, bring to mind these different ways of relating to the situation, and see what happens.'

'What's the worst that can happen right?' said Hare.

'Precisely. You may find that you can more calmly handle whatever it is that's on your plate, and you may just be able to appreciate some of the benefits of uncertainty.

Hare nodded, feeling that this had been a very productive session.

'Finally Hare, remember we did the mindful exercise? This can help you drop the struggle and embrace the unknown.'

ENDINGS

Hare had started to look forward to his CBT sessions with Crow. Five weeks had passed and he was feeling better about himself. Hare had always been a goal-orientated animal and the small homework tasks being set each week had helped him structure his days. His five minutes of movement sometimes turned into a stroll around the village. Brushing and bathing became routine again. He had even cooked for Harriet one evening. His mood was improving.

'Hello Hare.'

'Hello Crow.' Hare smiled.

'How are you feeling now that today is our last session?'

'Oh...there is no chance of continuing?'

'My work here is done Hare; you have come such a long way from when we first met. However, I feel there are some unresolved issues between you and your parents. I would like to put you in touch with Owl. He is a psychodynamic counsellor and his approach tends to focus on deeper issues.'

Hare's shoulders tensed up.

'Throughout our time together I have noticed some tension whenever we mention your parents. I wonder if there is more to this?'

'Yes, I feel there is... I am open to meeting Owl.'

'Being open is a wonderful trait, Hare.'

'Thank you.'

Crow ended the session and Hare left feeling nervous but excited to continue his journey.

4
TORTOISE

ONE MONTH AFTER THE RACE

One month after the race, Tortoise was still struggling with his sudden rise to fame. The animals greeted him wherever he went, he had been asked to give talks at schools and he had done many interviews.

However, the knot in his stomach was there when he woke up and remained there until he fell asleep. Since the race he had tried to talk about this knot with his mother and father, but they didn't quite seem to understand what Tortoise was going through.

One evening, Tortoise sat both his parents down. 'I think I should see a counsellor,' Tortoise said timidly.

'Okay Tortoise, if this is what you wish to do, we support you,' came his mother's response.

Tortoise's father smiled encouragingly. 'We are so proud of you son. I never expected you to win the race. I will be the first to admit I haven't been very supportive. But you haven't been yourself since the race. I think seeing someone about this might just be the way forward.'

Tearing up Tortoise had never felt so loved.

COUNSELLING BEGINNINGS WITH RAVEN

Tortoise had read up on how to find a counsellor. He read how it was important to have someone you could trust and to explore your feelings. He tried two counsellors prior to finding Raven. The first had exclaimed on the phone 'You beat Hare!' and had congratulated him on winning the race. The second explained there was a conflict of interest. Tortoise understood if a counsellor was seeing someone Tortoise had links too, they could not work together. Also, if what Tortoise might say in a session was likely to be something which could cause the counsellor an unhelpful emotional response known as countertransference this would not be helpful and would result in a conflict in interest. This would mean that the counsellor was not the right match to this therapy subject.

'Hello Tortoise, my name is Raven, and I am a humanistic counsellor. Each session will be fifty-five minutes. Would you like to know a bit about how I work?'

'Yes please,' replied Tortoise.

'So, I work within the three core conditions: empathy, congruence and unconditional positive regard. There is no judgement within this safe space and everything you say will remain private and confidential.'

Tortoise nodded.

Raven continued, 'This will only breakdown if you are planning on seriously hurting yourself or if you are planning on seriously hurting others. Is this something I should be concerned about?'

Tortoise paused before replying. 'No...'

'Any other questions?' asked Raven.

'Yes, what do you mean by empathy?'

'Empathy is where I will be joining you with your thoughts, feelings and emotions. It will be the respect I hold for you, noting that your experiences may be different to mine.'

'So, would it be like walking in my shoes?'

'Yes and what that feels like for you.'

Tortoise's heart sank. 'Will you feel sorry for me then?'

'No, Tortoise. Sympathy may lead to pity and pity would make a victim of the sufferer. Empathy, on the other hand, empowers you. With empathy, I get a sense of your world, you are not alone, and we will go through this together.' Raven smiled at Tortoise, letting him know that everything was going to be alright.

Tortoise felt the honesty in Raven's look. 'I like the sound of that. And congruence ... this means you will be genuine?'

'Yes, Tortoise, I will be authentic. Together, we will develop a relationship based on trust.' Raven saw Tortoise's shoulders relax a little. 'Are we okay to continue?'

'Yes.'

'Okay then. Let us begin.'

Raven established the therapeutic relationship with Tortoise with ease. Her body language was neutral, her voice warm and Tortoise felt safe. Raven listened as Tortoise explained his story. Not once did Raven move the conversation onto another topic and she did not lead it in another direction. Only occasionally she reflected back what Tortoise had said or asking a question to clarify something.

'I don't know how to get rid of this knot.' Tortoise concluded.

Silence.

'Okay Tortoise, let me summarise. This knot has been with you since the race and you've been to the doctor, but they've found nothing wrong with you physically. You have a fear that this knot is psychological and it is now affecting your everyday life. You would like to get rid of the knot but are not sure how.'

Tortoise was surprised at how Raven had been able to sum up the forty-five minutes of their conversation into three short sentences.

'Do you know how I can get rid of it?' Tortoise looked at Raven with hope.

'You might not know it now, but with time you will know the answer yourself,' said Raven, smiling.

'But, if you had this knot, what would you do?' Tortoise sounded desperate.

'Every individual is unique. A one-size-fits-all answer would not, in fact, fit all. The way I might do it may not work for you. Your own experience will be the most vital factor in the process to resolve your current feelings.'

Tortoise pondered on what Raven had just said. 'I have the answer within?'

'I believe you do.'

Tortoise felt brave.

'We have reached the end of our session, would you like us to continue next week, Tortoise?'

'Thank you, Raven.'

COUNSELLING MIDDLES

After a couple of sessions together Raven and Tortoise had developed a good working alliance. In today's session Raven felt Tortoise was ready to delve deeper.

'Describe this knot.'

'Most days it feels dark and constantly twisting. It feels big and heavy, always with me. It affects every part of my body. I feel … so … unworthy.' Tortoise felt flat, his shoulders drooped, head down. A heavy silence filled the room. Raven broke the silence as she sensed Tortoise slipping into darkness.

'You no longer feel worthy? Could you explain a little bit more?'

'I have never been a very confident creature, but since winning the race, my confidence has hit rock bottom. Imagine that! Winning the race that I've worked almost all of my life for and I'm feeling sorry for myself,' Tortoise laughed.

Raven knew it was common to mask raw emotion with humour and this was what Tortoise was doing. Tortoise, for sure, thought Raven would be laughing at him. But when he met her eyes, she was looking directly at him and for the first time in a long time, Tortoise felt really seen. He teared up with no shame.

Raven sat with Tortoise whilst he cried. It had reached the end of the session and Raven's only movement had been placing a box of tissues in front of him. Raven had not tried to take away Tortoise's struggles with soothing words or hugs. She simply sat with him through his pain and that was all that Tortoise wanted.

TORTOISE BRINGS UP THE RACE

Raven looked out of the small window. She looked forward to her sessions with Tortoise feeling he had made much progress. He was always on time and paid promptly. Right on time, there was a knock on the door.

'Come in.'

Raven watched Tortoise settle in his seat, for him to then stand up, then sit back down.

'Everything okay Tortoise? You seem agitated,' challenged Raven.

'I am ready to talk about the race,' Tortoise said boldly.

'Okay.' Raven patted her knees. 'I feel this is a subject we have been skirting around, where would you like to start?'

'After the race.'

'Okay, could you tell me how you felt after the race Tortoise?'

'I felt I had masses of adrenaline, I was buzzing, but that quickly plummeted, and my energy crashed and the knot in my stomach formed. I couldn't sleep that night, nor the next night … nor the one after that.'

Raven allowed the space for Tortoise to continue.

'I felt so anxious, but I didn't – still don't, understand why. When I became anxious about the knot, and about the anxiety itself, it became even worse.'

'So, would you say you developed a fear around the anxiety?'

'I would. A real sense of unease.'

Raven looked thoughtful before saying, 'Anxiety is irrational, it can feel like you have no control and this can leave you feeling really helpless.'

Tortoise nodded.

'This knot in your stomach … is it physical?'

Silence.

'Tortoise I notice you are looking very tense?' Raven said, using a Gestalt-style question. Gestalt was a practitioner who picked up body language in counselling.

'I feel very tense. If I focus on it, I break out in a sweat, my breathing becomes quick. Just talking about it, I feel my heartbeat quickening.'

Raven noticed how panicked Tortoise looked and wondered whether his behaviour might lead into a panic attack.

'Tortoise, listen to my voice. Feel the ground beneath your feet. Now, bring attention to your breath, focus on a long inhale and a long exhale. Breathe.'

Tortoise did as he was told. Once Raven felt Tortoise looked calmer, she went on, 'Anxiety can be very fear based and studies have shown high anxiety can affect brain structures like the Amygdala which causes the physical affects you are experiencing now.'

'Amygdala?'

'The Amygdala is a small part located in the centre of the brain,' said Raven.

'What is the difference between dealing with stress and dealing with anxiety?' asked Tortoise.

'Stress can sometimes be dealt with by relaxation whereas anxiety sometimes needs a stronger intervention. Stress is very much happening right now, whereas anxiety is over things in the past and in an imagined future.'

'Yes, ever since the race I have been feeling anxious,' said Tortoise.

'Mm,' nodded Raven.

'How do you see my anxiety Raven?'

'This anxiety is something we can look at, breakdown, so we can let you grow to your full potential.'

'How?'

'I provide the space and you hold the key,' said Raven, smiling. 'You have your own unique set of circumstances. With this real contact between you and myself, the anxiety can be lifted as you start to experience self-acceptance and self-worth.'

'I feel like I am slowly healing the more I talk about this knot, which I now understand as anxiety.'

Raven smiled encouragingly.

Tortoise went on, 'I accept how I am feeling at this moment, I surrender to it and I feel it's pain.'

Raven understood this as a very powerful moment.

'I felt guilty for winning the race, as if I didn't deserve it and have suffered ever since.'

'You have shared a lot today Tortoise, how are you feeling?'

'Better.' Tortoise smiled.

SHAME

Tortoise found that when he heard some of his own words repeated back to him, he could self-edit and clarify what he meant. This happened occasionally with Raven, sometimes he would correct her several times, until Tortoise decided that he had expressed exactly what he was thinking and how he felt. He thought that he often rambled but Raven always brought things back to the present moment.

Raven was aware Tortoise felt great shame for winning the race. She also knew that too much support could be disabling and too little could be unhelpful.

'What is the root of you feeling unworthy Tortoise?'

Tortoise hesitated. Raven realised she could have triggered the shame and may have not provided enough relational support.

'Did I say something that disturbed you?'

'Yes.'

There was a long silence. An elephant in the room.

'Shame is the root,' said Tortoise quietly.

'Ah, shame is experienced by those who feel fundamentally unacceptable, unworthy which can lead to a desperate urge to disappear.'

'It feels so overwhelming. I feel a loss of myself.'

'Let us try to normalise the shame you have experienced Tortoise. Tell me, what is shame?'

'It is a feeling.'

'Yes, another feeling that can be faced and worked through.'

'Just saying it out loud makes me feel relief.' Tortoise sighed.

'So, Tortoise, how are you feeling now?'

'Better within myself, Raven.'

The humanistic-focused process facilitated Tortoise's self-discovery, self-acceptance, and provided a way towards healing and growth.

COUNSELLING ENDINGS

Throughout the weeks Tortoise had worked hard on himself. During his counselling sessions with Raven and outside of his counselling sessions too. He had explored his values, his relationships and observed how he interacted with the other animals. He found himself no longer seeking validation from Raven, his parents or friends and was becoming more assertive in his life choices.

In his next counselling session, he said honestly, 'I don't think I ever want our sessions to end, Raven.'

'Tortoise let me explain the importance of endings in terms of tidying a messy cupboard.'

'Okay.'

'We have been pulling everything out and we have been sifting through it, keeping the things that are useful to you and placing them back. Do you feel we have placed everything back?'

'Mm, the knot has come apart. We have broken it down and it now holds no power over me. The cupboard is my mind, is that correct? My mind certainly feels much better.'

Raven smiled and Tortoise smiled back.

'You feel it, don't you?' said Raven.

'Yes, I do. I feel ready' replied Tortoise.

'So, are we in mutual agreement that next week should be our last session?'

'Yes.' Tortoise knew it was time.

Tortoise and Raven spent the rest of the session talking about Tortoise's previous endings and if they had been positive or negative. Afterwards Tortoise left the session feeling prepared that the next week would be his last session.

THE LAST COUNSELLING ENDING

'So, Tortoise, how are you feeling?'

'Sad this is coming to end, a bit scared actually, but I am feeling good about myself.'

'When experienced well, endings need no longer be feared, but embraced as an intrinsic part of animal experience.'

'When one door closes, another opens.' Tortoise beamed out a toothy smile.

'Yes, Tortoise,' Raven nodded back, mirroring Tortoise's delight.

5
MEETING OWL

OWL THE PSYCHODYNAMIC COUNSELLOR

Hare lay on his back. Owl was seated out of his line of sight.

'Good morning Hare, I understand you have been referred to me by CBT counsellor Crow. She seems to believe some issues are rooted deeper. I am here to explore these issues.'

Hare felt nervous. Owl was much more serious looking than Crow.

'Hare, we are going to a free association exercise, a common technique we use where you will respond with whatever comes to your mind.'

'Okay...'

Owl said, 'Growing up?'

'I was in a family of six, it was a very busy house, but my mother and father always helped each of us pursue our goals.'

'Try not to think, keep it short,' said Owl.

'Okay. Family of six," replied Hare.

'Siblings?', questioned Owl

'I spent most of my time looking after the youngest, Harriet.'

'Parents?,' said Owl.

'Busy,' said Hare.

'Family values?,' said Owl.

Hare said, 'Winning.'

'Winning?' Owl questioned.

Hare went on. 'It was tough having older brothers and sisters, I always worked extra hard to get my parent's attention. My siblings all excelled academically or in sports. I really struggled at times but winning earnt my parent's respect.'

Silence.

'Is my childhood important?' Hare asked, timidly.

'One's personality can be firmly rooted in your childhood experience. To truly address your issues, we must dig deep into your unconscious. This is where we store our unspoken values, the beliefs we do not even realise we have and the patterns of thought and behaviour developed in childhood.'

Silence.

'What do you truly believe Hare?'

'I believe if I don't win races, my parents will not acknowledge me.'

'Acknowledge you?'

'They won't see me ...'

Silence.

'I have many siblings, I always felt the need to win, so they can see me and be proud of me.'

'By winning races, you feel seen?'

'Yes.'

'Okay Hare, our time has come to an end, are you happy to proceed next week, same time and place?'

'Yes.'

Hare left Owl's room in a bit of a daze. Had he really said all of that out loud? He felt very exposed. Hare always felt he came across as strong and confident, yet in one session he had let his guard down and revealed his deepest fear.

DREAMS

That night Hare had a dream. It was Christmas and father was making a toast to his family, congratulating each child one by one for something they had achieved that year. When it came to Hare, father paused.

'… and to my son Hare … for losing the race to Tortoise and making a mockery of the family!'

Hare woke up. He went into the kitchen and poured himself a glass of water. He remembered that Christmas. His father hadn't mentioned him in his family toast. Hare had always wondered if father had forgotten about him.

DREAM ANALYSIS

'I can't stop dreaming,' Hare said, lying on the couch.

'Tell me about your dream.'

Hare did not know where to start. 'What would you like to know?'

'What are the materials of a dream and how do these materials work together?' asked Owl.

'But, why are dreams important?'

'Combinations of dream elements are not random but rather guided by emotion; accordingly, dreams are helpful for building and rebuilding an individual's emotional memory system. In brief, emotions are likely to play the role of order parameters: they control and guide combinations of dream elements.' Owl explained.

'Emotions can, therefore, serve as a springboard in comprehending dreams. For instance, perhaps traumatic experiences constitute a core theme of a patient's dreams, suggesting an avenue for further treatment.'

'So, you can derive important information from what is in my dreams and you can grasp the core of a dream?'

'Yes precisely,' said Owl. He was impressed how quickly Hare cottoned on.

'My father usually does not acknowledge me at the family dinners, but this time he did. He said I had brought shame to the family for losing the race.'

'Sounds traumatic.'

'Yes.' Hare sighed. 'Owl, I am tired, may we end the session early?'

'As you wish Hare.'

PSYCHOANALYSIS OF FREUD

'Your diagnosis was originally depression Hare; can I share a theory?

'Yes,' Hare replied, shuffling his body in closer.

'From a Freudian perspective, depression is understood as an experience of loss or rejection by a parent.'

'So, you are saying depression is like a form of grief for a relationship that never was?'

'Yes Hare, rather than expressing your frustrations you have turned your sadness inward.'

Hare nodded.

'You have thought of yourself as worthless. As a child, a depressive animal learned that their parents' care was not readily available.'

Hare thought back to the times as a small child he had felt ignored by his parents. Hare felt angry. As if reading Hare's emotions Owl went on to ask, 'did you feel angry as a child Hare?'

'I did but I could never voice this from fear of being completely ignored.'

'Ah yes, the fear of abandonment.'

Hare nodded.

'But, because you were unable to express them, you internalised your feelings, and you might have felt unworthy of their love or felt you were a bad animal.'

Hare said, 'I tried hard in my studies, in my running ...'

'To gain their love,' finished Owl.

'Yes,' said Hare.

'If their love was not forthcoming, you may have felt you would never be good enough, no matter how hard you tried.'

Hare started to sob. He realised it was time to confront his parents and express his pain.

6
NEW BEGINNINGS

Walking through the woods, Hare noticed the leaves changing colour. Things were much better with his parents and he continued to see Owl once a week. He stopped, looked at the sky, a ray of sunlight beamed onto his face. He took in the warmth with his heart and arms wide open. As Hare looked ahead, he saw Tortoise strolling towards him. Their eyes met, and they shared a knowing smile before carrying on their separate ways.

REFERENCES

Anxiety and Depression Association of America., (2010-2018). *Understand the Facts: Stress* [online]. Anxiety and Depression Association of America. [Viewed March 2020]. Available from: https://adaa.org/understanding-anxiety/related-illnesses/stress

Butler-Bowdon, T., (2006). *50 Psychology Classics: Who We Are, How We Think, What We Do*. Nicholas Brealey Publishing.

Dierks, A. (2016). *Approaches to Working with Depression* [online]. Counselling Directory. [Viewed March 2020]. Available from: https://www.counselling-directory.org.uk/memberarticles/approaches-to-working-with-depression

Joyce, P. and Sills, C., (2018). *Skills in Gestalt Counselling & Psychotherapy*. 4th ed. SAGE Publications Ltd.

SimplyPsychology. *Psychology Articles for Students* [Viewed March 2020]. Available from: https://www.simplypsychology.org

ABOUT THE AUTHOR

Maria 彗 Claridge is half English half Japanese and was born in Lymington. She wrote this book whilst studying to become a counsellor, with the intention of helping people understand the different types of counselling and what techniques are used. Her interest stemmed from always wondering what happened to the Hare and the Tortoise after the race.

Printed in Great Britain
by Amazon